1×1

Books by E. E. Cummings

The Enormous Room (1922)

Tulips and Chimneys (1923)

& [AND] (1925)

XLI Poems (1925)

is 5 (1926)

Him (1927)

By E. E. Cummings (1930)

CIOPW (1931)

W [ViVa] (1931)

Eimi (1933)

No Thanks (1933)

Tom (1935)

Collected Poems (1938)

50 Poems (1940)

1 x 1 (1944)

Anthropos: The Future of Art (1945)

Santa Claus (1946)

Xaipe (1950)

i: six nonlectures (1953)

Poems: 1923–1954 (1954)

A Miscellany (1958)

95 Poems (1958)

Adventures in Value (with Marion Morehouse) (1962)

73 Poems (1963)

Fairy Tales (1965)

E. E. Cummings: A Selection of Poems (1965)

Complete Poems 1913–1962 (1972)

E. E. CUMMINGS

1 × 1

A Harvest/HBJ Book
Harcourt Brace Jovanovich
New York and London

Library of Congress Number 54-10935

ISBN 0-15-668800-X

Printed in the United States of America

C D E F G H I J

INDEX OF FIRST LINES

ACKNOWLEDGMENTS

Certain of these poems first appeared in the pages of *Poetry: A Magazine of Verse*, *Accent*, *Harper's Bazaar*, *Furioso*, and the *Quarterly Review of Literature*.

The following poems were published in *View:* VII, VIII, IX, X, XI, XIV, XXVII, XL.

1

nonsun blob a
cold to
skylessness
sticking fire

my are your
are birds our all
and one gone
away the they

leaf of ghosts some
few creep there
here or on
unearth

neither could say
(it comes so slow
not since not why)
both didn't know

exeunt they
(not false not true
not you not i)
it comes so who

it's over a(see just
over this)wall
the apples are(yes
they're gravensteins)all
as red as to lose
and as round as to find.

Each why of a leaf says
(floating each how)
you're which as to die
(each green of a new)
you're who as to grow
but you're he as to do

what must(whispers)be must
be(the wise fool)
if living's to give
so breathing's to steal—
five wishes are five
and one hand is a mind

then over our thief goes
(you go and i)
has pulled(for he's we)
such fruit from what bough
that someone called they
made him pay with his now.

But over a(see just
over this)wall
the red and the round
(they're gravensteins)fall
with kind of a blind
big sound on the ground

III

of all the blessings which to man
kind progress doth impart
one stands supreme i mean the an
imal without a heart.

Huge this collective pseudobeast
(sans either pain or joy)
does nothing except preexist
its hoi in its polloi

and if sometimes he's prodded forth
to exercise her vote
(or made by threats of something worth
than death to change their coat

—which something as you'll never guess
in fifty thousand years
equals the quote and unquote loss
of liberty my dears—

or even is compelled to fight
itself from tame to teem)
still doth our hero contemplate
in raptures of undream

that strictly(and how)scienti
fic land of supernod
where freedom is compulsory
and only man is god.

Without a heart the animal
is very very kind
so kind it wouldn't like a soul
and couldn't use a mind

IV

squints a blond
job at her
diamond
solitaire

while guesswho nibbles his ton of torse

squirms a pool
of pink fat
screams a hole
in it

that birth was wicked and life is worse

squats a big
dove on g
w's wig
so what he

is much too busy sitting the horse

my(his from daughter's mother's zero mind
fahrenheit)old infrequently more and
more much(as aprils elsewhere stroll)exhumed

most innocently undecaying friend
hangs at yon gilty ceiling per both pale
orbs thus excluding a leanderless

drowning in sub(at the next)nakedness
(table but three)hero's carnivorous(smile
by lipstick smell by matchabelli)tits

as(while thumb a plus fingers all with blind
him of who)i discreetly(masturbates
one honest breadcrumb)say "i understand

quite what you mean by"
                        sold!to the dollarfull shea
with a weakness for living literature
                              "loyaltea"

ygUDuh

    ydoan
    yunnuhstan

    ydoan o
    yunnuhstan dem
    yguduh ged

    yunnuhstan dem doidee
    yguduh ged riduh
    ydoan o nudn
LISN bud LISN

        dem
        gud
        am

        lidl yelluh bas
        tuds weer goin

duhSIVILEYEzum

applaws)

"fell
ow
sit
isn'ts"

(a paw s

a salesman is an it that stinks Excuse

Me whether it's president of the you were say
or a jennelman name misder finger isn't
important whether it's millions of other punks
or just a handful absolutely doesn't
matter and whether it's in lonjewray

or shrouds is immaterial it stinks

a salesman is an it that stinks to please

but whether to please itself or someone else
makes no more difference than if it sells
hate condoms education snakeoil vac
uumcleaners terror strawberries democ
ra(caveat emptor)cy superfluous hair

or Think We've Met subhuman rights Before

a politician is an arse upon
which everyone has sat except a man

mr u will not be missed
who as an anthologist
sold the many on the few
not excluding mr u

it was a goodly co
which paid to make man free
(for man is enslaved by a dread dizziz
and the sooner it's over the sooner to biz
don't ask me what it's pliz)

then up rose bishop budge from kew
a anglican was who
(with a rag and a bone and a hank of hair)'d
he picked up a thousand pounds or two
and he smote the monster merde

then up rose pride and up rose pelf
and ghibelline and guelph
and ladios and laddios
(on radios and raddios)
did save man from himself

ye duskiest despot's goldenest gal
did wring that dragon's tail
(for men must loaf and women must lay)
and she gave him a desdemonial
that took his breath away

all history oped her teeming womb
said demon for to doom
yea(fresh complexions being oke
with him)one william shakespeare broke
the silence of the tomb

then up rose mr lipshits pres
(who always nothing says)
and he kisséd the general menedjerr
and they smokéd a robert burns cigerr
to the god of things like they err

plato told

him:he couldn't
believe it(jesus

told him;he
wouldn't believe
it)lao

tsze
certainly told
him,and general
(yes

mam)
sherman;
and even
(believe it
or

not)you
told him:i told
him;we told him
(he didn't believe it,no

sir)it took
a nipponized bit of
the old sixth

avenue
el;in the top of his head:to tell

him

XIII

pity this busy monster,manunkind,

not.   Progress is a comfortable disease:
your victim(death and life safely beyond)

plays with the bigness of his littleness
—electrons deify one razorblade
into a mountainrange;lenses extend

unwish through curving wherewhen till unwish
returns on its unself.
                      A world of made
is not a world of born—pity poor flesh

and trees,poor stars and stones,but never this
fine specimen of hypermagical

ultraomnipotence.   We doctors know

a hopeless case if—listen:there's a hell
of a good universe next door;let's go

("fire stop thief help murder save the world"

what world?
            is it themselves these insects mean?
when microscopic shriekings shall have snarled
threads of celestial silence huger than
eternity,men will be saviours
                    —flop
grasshopper,exactly nothing's soon;
scream,all ye screamers,till your if is up
and vanish under prodigies of un)

"have you" the mountain,while his maples wept
air to blood,asked "something a little child
who's just as small as me can do or be?"
god whispered him a snowflake "yes:you may
sleep now,my mountain" and this mountain slept

while his pines lifted their green lives and smiled

one's not half two. It's two are halves of one:
which halves reintegrating,shall occur
no death and any quantity;but than
all numerable mosts the actual more

minds ignorant of stern miraculous
this every truth—beware of heartless them
(given the scalpel,they dissect a kiss;
or,sold the reason,they undream a dream)

one is the song which fiends and angels sing:
all murdering lies by mortals told make two.
Let liars wilt,repaying life they're loaned;
we(by a gift called dying born)must grow

deep in dark least ourselves remembering
love only rides his year.
                              All lose,whole find

X

one(Floatingly)arrive

(silent)one by(alive)
from(into disappear

and perfectly)nowhere
vivid anonymous
mythical guests of Is

unslowly more who(and
here who there who)descend
-ing(mercifully)touch
deathful earth's any which

Weavingly now one by
wonder(on twilight)they
come until(over dull

all nouns)begins a whole
verbal adventure to

illimitably Grow

as any(men's hells having wrestled with)
man drops into his own paradise
thankfully
                whole and the green whereless truth
of an eternal now welcomes each was
of whom among not numerable ams

(leaving a perfectly distinct unhe;
a ticking phantom by prodigious time's
mere brain contrived:a spook of stop and go)
may i achieve another steepest thing—

how more than sleep illimitably my
—being so very born no bird can sing
as easily creation up all sky

(really unreal world,will you perhaps do
the breathing for me while i am away?)

XVIII

when you are silent,shining host by guest
a snowingly enfolding glory is

all angry common things to disappear
causing through mystery miracle peace:

or(if begin the colours of your voice)
from some complete existence of to dream
into complete some dream of to exist
a stranger who is i awakening am.

Living no single thing dares partly seem
one atomy once,and every cannot stir
imagining;while you are motionless—

whose moving is more april than the year
(if all her most first little flowers rise

out of tremendous darkness into air)

XIX

what if a much of a which of a wind
gives the truth to summer's lie;
bloodies with dizzying leaves the sun
and yanks immortal stars awry?
Blow king to beggar and queen to seem
(blow friend to fiend:blow space to time)
—when skies are hanged and oceans drowned,
the single secret will still be man

what if a keen of a lean wind flays
screaming hills with sleet and snow:
strangles valleys by ropes of thing
and stifles forests in white ago?
Blow hope to terror;blow seeing to blind
(blow pity to envy and soul to mind)
—whose hearts are mountains,roots are trees,
it's they shall cry hello to the spring

what if a dawn of a doom of a dream
bites this universe in two,
peels forever out of his grave
and sprinkles nowhere with me and you?
Blow soon to never and never to twice
(blow life to isn't:blow death to was)
—all nothing's only our hugest home;
the most who die,the more we live

XX

dead every enormous piece
of nonsense which itself must call
a state submicroscopic is—
compared with pitying terrible
some alive individual

ten centuries of original soon
or make it ten times ten are more
than not entitled to complain
—plunged in eternal now if who're
by the five nevers of a lear

no man,if men are gods;but if gods must
be men,the sometimes only man is this
(most common,for each anguish is his grief;
and,for his joy is more than joy,most rare)

a fiend,if fiends speak truth;if angels burn

by their own generous completely light,
an angel;or(as various worlds he'll spurn
rather than fail immeasurable fate)
coward,clown,traitor,idiot,dreamer,beast—

such was a poet and shall be and is

—who'll solve the depths of horror to defend
a sunbeam's architecture with his life:
and carve immortal jungles of despair
to hold a mountain's heartbeat in his hand

love is a spring at which
crazy they drink who've climbed
steeper than hopes are fears
only not ever named
mountains more if than each
known allness disappears

lovers are mindless they
higher than fears are hopes
lovers are those who kneel
lovers are these whose lips
smash unimagined sky
deeper than heaven is hell

(once like a spark)

if strangers meet
life begins—
not poor not rich
(only aware)
kind neither
nor cruel
(only complete)
i not not you
not possible;
only truthful
—truthfully,once
if strangers(who
deep our most are
selves)touch:
forever

(and so to dark)

XXIV

what over and which under
burst lurch things phantoms curl
(mouth seekingly lips wander
a finding whom of girl)

dolls clutching their dolls wallow
toys playing writhe with toys
(than are all unworlds hollow
silence has deeper eyes

purest than fear's obscener
brightest than hate's more black
keenest than dying's keener
each will kissed breast awake)

slow tottering visions bigly
come crashing into go
(all than were nevers ugly
beautiful most is now)

when god decided to invent
everything he took one
breath bigger than a circustent
and everything began

when man determined to destroy
himself he picked the was
of shall and finding only why
smashed it into because

old mr ly
fresh from a fu
ruddy as a sun
with blue true two

man
neral
rise
eyes

"this world's made 'bout
right it's the people that
abuses it you can git
anything you like out

of it if
you gut a mind
to there's something
for everybody it's a"

old mr lyman
ruddy as a sunrise
fresh with blue come
true from

a funeral
eyes
"big
thing"

XXVII

rain or hail
sam done
the best he kin
till they digged his hole

:sam was a man

stout as a bridge
rugged as a bear
slickern a weazel
how be you

(sun or snow)

gone into what
like all them kings
you read about
and on him sings

a whippoorwill;

heart was big
as the world aint square
with room for the devil
and his angels too

yes,sir

what may be better
or what may be worse
and what may be clover
clover clover

(nobody'll know)

sam was a man
grinned his grin
done his chores
laid him down.

Sleep well

let it go—the
smashed word broken
open vow or
the oath cracked length
wise—let it go it
was sworn to
        go

let them go—the
truthful liars and
the false fair friends
and the boths and
neithers—you must let them go they
were born
        to go

let all go—the
big small middling
tall bigger really
the biggest and all
things—let all go
dear
     so comes love

XXIX

Hello is what a mirror says
it is a maid says Who
and(hearing not a which)replies
in haste I must be you

no sunbeam ever lies

Bang is the meaning of a gun
it is a man means No
and(seeing something yes)will grin
with pain You so&so

true wars are never won

a-

float on some
?
i call twilight you

'll see

an in
-ch
of an if

&

who
is
the

)

more
dream than become
more

am than imagine

i've come to ask you if there isn't a
new moon outside your window saying if

that's all,just if"
                    "that's all there is to say"

(and she looked)"especially in winter"(like a leaf
opening)
            as we stood,one(truthed
by wisping tinily the silverest

alive silentness god ever breathed

upon beginning)
                    "beautiful o most
beautiful" her,my life worships and
(night)
            then "everything beautiful can grow"

my,her life marvels "here'll be a canoe

and a whole world and then a single hair
again" marvels "and liars kill their kind

but" her,my "love creates love only" our

XXXII

open green those
(dear)
worlds of than great
more eyes,and what
were summer's beside their
glories

downward if they'll
or
goldenly float
so(dreaming out
of dreams among)no year
will fall

this than,a least
dare
of snow less quite
is nothing but
herself,and than this(mere
most)breast

spring's million(who
are
and do not wait)
buds imitate
upward each first flower
of two

XXXIII

nothing false and possible is love
(who's imagined,therefore limitless)
love's to giving as to keeping's give;
as yes is to if,love is to yes

must's a schoolroom in the month of may:
life's the deathboard where all now turns when
(love's a universe beyond obey
or command,reality or un-)

proudly depths above why's first because
(faith's last doubt and humbly heights below)
kneeling,we—true lovers—pray that us
will ourselves continue to outgrow

all whose mosts if you have known and i've
only we our least begin to guess

except in your
honour,
my loveliest,
nothing
may move may rest
—you bring

(out of dark the
earth)a
procession of
wonders
huger than prove
our fears

were hopes:the moon
open
for you and close
will shy
wings of because;
each why

of star(afloat
on not
quite less than all
of time)
gives you skilful
his flame

so is your heart
alert,
of languages
there's none
but well she knows;
and can

perfectly speak
(snowflake
and rainbow mind
and soul
november and
april)

who younger than
begin
are,the worlds move
in your
(and rest,my love)
honour

true lovers in each happening of their hearts
live longer than all which and every who;
despite what fear denies,what hope asserts,
what falsest both disprove by proving true

(all doubts,all certainties,as villains strive
and heroes through the mere mind's poor pretend
—grim comics of duration:only love
immortally occurs beyond the mind)

such a forever is love's any now
and her each here is such an everywhere,
even more true would truest lovers grow
if out of midnight dropped more suns than are

(yes;and if time should ask into his was
all shall,their eyes would never miss a yes)

XXXVI

we love each other very dearly
                              ,more
than raindrops need sunbeams or snowflakes make
possible mayflowers:

                    quite eyes of air
not with twilight's first thrushes may awake
more secretly than our(if disappear
should some world)selves

                         .No doing shall undo
(nor madness nor mere death nor both who is
la guerre)your me or simplify my you
,darling

        sweet this creative never known
complexity was born before the moon
before God wished Himself into a rose

and even(
          we'll adventure the into
most immemorial of whens
)before

each heartbeat which i am alive to kiss

yes is a pleasant country:
if's wintry
(my lovely)
let's open the year

both is the very weather
(not either)
my treasure,
when violets appear

love is a deeper season
than reason;
my sweet one
(and april's where we're)

all ignorance toboggans into know
and trudges up to ignorance again:
but winter's not forever,even snow
melts;and if spring should spoil the game,what then?

all history's a winter sport or three:
but were it five,i'd still insist that all
history is too small for even me;
for me and you,exceedingly too small.

Swoop(shrill collective myth)into thy grave
merely to toil the scale to shrillerness
per every madge and mabel dick and dave
—tomorrow is our permanent address

and there they'll scarcely find us(if they do,
we'll move away still further:into now

darling!because my blood can sing
and dance(and does with each your least
your any most very amazing now
or here)let pitiless fear play host
to every isn't that's under the spring
—but if a look should april me,
down isn't's own isn't go ghostly they

doubting can turn men's see to stare
their faith to how their joy to why
their stride and breathing to limp and prove
—but if a look should april me,
some thousand million hundred more
bright worlds than merely by doubting have
darkly themselves unmade makes love

armies(than hate itself and no
meanness unsmaller)armies can
immensely meet for centuries
and(except nothing)nothing's won
—but if a look should april me
for half a when,whatever is less
alive than never begins to yes

but if a look should april me
(though such as perfect hope can feel
only despair completely strikes
forests of mind,mountains of soul)
quite at the hugest which of his who
death is killed dead.   Hills jump with brooks:
trees tumble out of twigs and sticks;

1

how

tinily
of

squir(two be
tween sto
nes)ming a gr

eenes
t you b
ecome

s whi
(mysterious
ly)te

one
t

hou

might these be thrushes climbing through almost(do they

beautifully wandering in merciful
miracles wonderingly celebrate day
and welcome earth's arrival with a soul)

sunlight? yes
                (always we have heard them sing
the dark alive but)
                        look:begins to grow
more than all real,all imagining;

and we who are we? surely not i not you
behold nor any breathing creature this?
nothing except the impossible shall occur

—see!now himself uplifts of stars the star
(sing!every joy)—wholly now disappear
night's not eternal terrors like a guess.

Life's life and strikes my your our blossoming sphere

XLII

if(among
silent skies
bluer than believing)a
little gay
earth opening
is all the flowers of his eyes
: april's they

this if now
or this(young
trembling any)into flame
twig or limb
explodes and o
each living ablaze greenly thing
; may has come

love(by yes
every new
bird no bigger than to sing)
leaf is wing
and tree is voice
more leastfully than i am you
, we are spring

these(whom;pretends

blue nothing)
are
built of soon carved
of to born of
be

One

:petals
him starrily her
and around
ing swim
snowing

ly upward with Joy,

no
where(no)when
may
breathe
so sky so

.wish

XLIV

i think you like"

a strawberry
bang this
blueeyed world(on
which are wintry

handlebars

glued)updives pursued
by its wigglesome whisperful
body and
almost

isn't(grabbed into skies of

grin)"my
flowers"(the humble
man than sunlight
older with ships than

dreams more hands are

offering jonquils)down again
who but zooms
through
one perfectly beautiful bow

"my home ionian isles

open your heart:
i'll give you a treasure
of tiniest world
a piece of forever with

summitless younger than
angels are mountains
rivery forests
towerful towns(queen

poet king float
sprout heroes of moonstar
flutter to and
swim blossoms of person)through

musical shadows while hunted
by daemons
seethe luminous
leopards(on wingfeet of thingfear)

come ships go
snowily sailing
perfect silence. Absolute ocean

XLVI

until and i heard
a certain a bird
i dreamed i could sing
but like nothing
                           are the joys
of his voice

until and who came
with a song like a dream
of a bird with a song
like not anything
                           under skies
over grass

until and until
into flame i can feel
how the earth must fly
if a truth is a cry
                           of a whole
of a soul

until i awoke
for the beautiful sake
of a grave gay brave
bright cry of alive
                           with a trill
like until

XLVII

so isn't small one littlest why,
it into if shall climb all the
blue heaven green earth neither sea
here's more than room for three of me

and only while your sweet eyes close
have disappeared a million whys;
but opening if are those eyes
every because is murdered twice

XLVIII

trees
        were in(give
give)bud when to me
you
made for by love
love said did
o no yes

earth was in
                (live
live)spring
with all beautiful
things when to
me
you gave gave darling

birds are
        in(trees are in)
song
when to me you
leap and i'm born we
're sunlight of
oneness

XLIX

which is the very
(in sad this havingest
world)most merry
most fair most rare
—the livingest givingest
girl on this whirlingest
earth?
        why you're
by far the darlingest

who(on this busily
nowhere rollingest
it)'s the dizzily
he most him
—the climbingly fallingest
fool in this trickiest
if?
    why i'm
by much the luckiest

what of the wonder
(beingest growingest)
over all under
all hate all fear
—all perfectly dyingest
my and foreverless
thy?
        why our
is love and neverless

"sweet spring is your
time is my time is our
time for springtime is lovetime
and viva sweet love"

(all the merry little birds are
flying in the floating in the
very spirits singing in
are winging in the blossoming)

lovers go and lovers come
awandering awondering
but any two are perfectly
alone there's nobody else alive

(such a sky and such a sun
i never knew and neither did you
and everybody never breathed
quite so many kinds of yes)

not a tree can count his leaves
each herself by opening
but shining who by thousands mean
only one amazing thing

(secretly adoring shyly
tiny winging darting floating
merry in the blossoming
always joyful selves are singing)

"sweet spring is your
time is my time is our
time for springtime is lovetime
and viva sweet love"

life is more true than reason will deceive
(more secret or than madness did reveal)
deeper is life than lose:higher than have
—but beauty is more each than living's all

multiplied with infinity sans if
the mightiest meditations of mankind
cancelled are by one merely opening leaf
(beyond whose nearness there is no beyond)

or does some littler bird than eyes can learn
look up to silence and completely sing?
futures are obsolete;pasts are unborn
(here less than nothing's more than everything)

death,as men call him,ends what they call men
—but beauty is more now than dying's when

o by the by
has anybody seen
little you-i
who stood on a green
hill and threw
his wish at blue

with a swoop and a dart
out flew his wish
(it dived like a fish
but it climbed like a dream)
throbbing like a heart
singing like a flame

blue took it my
far beyond far
and high beyond high
bluer took it your
but bluest took it our
away beyond where

what a wonderful thing
is the end of a string
(murmurs little you-i
as the hill becomes nil)
and will somebody tell
me why people let go

if everything happens that can't be done
(and anything's righter
than books
could plan)
the stupidest teacher will almost guess
(with a run
skip
around we go yes)
there's nothing as something as one

one hasn't a why or because or although
(and buds know better
than books
don't grow)
one's anything old being everything new
(with a what
which
around we come who)
one's everyanything so

so world is a leaf so tree is a bough
(and birds sing sweeter
than books
tell how)
so here is away and so your is a my
(with a down
up
around again fly)
forever was never till now

now i love you and you love me
(and books are shuter
than books
can be)
and deep in the high that does nothing but **fall**
(with a shout
each
around we go all)
there's somebody calling who's we

we're anything brighter than even the sun
(we're everything greater
than books
might mean)
we're everyanything more than believe
(with a spin
leap
alive we're alive)
we're wonderful one times one

marion's book